This book belongs to:

PICTURES & NOTES:

I Belong

Preparing for my First Holy Communion

PICTURES & NOTES:

Contents

We go to Sunday Mass. The chapters in
your book follow the framework of the Mass.

Stick a photo of yourself here and colour in the frame.

The journey begins

The first step of your journey to God was when you were baptised.

God said,

" alfie

you are my beloved child. I am delighted with you. "

Now you are older you are ready to make choices for yourself.
This book will help you belong to God's family by understanding
and taking part in the Mass.

**This year my family, my catechist and I will
get to know and love Jesus even more.**

**My catechist's
name is:**

I have a prayer sponsor who is praying for me.

**My prayer sponsor's
name is:**

Symbols used in this book

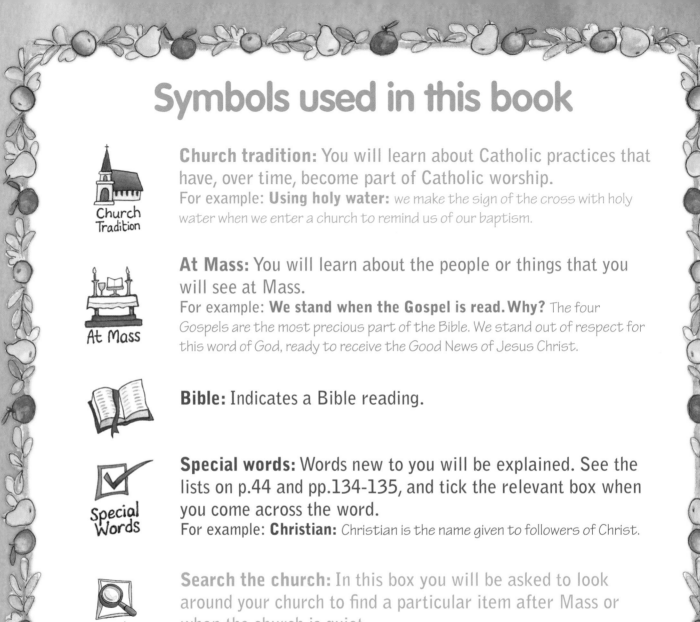

Church tradition: You will learn about Catholic practices that have, over time, become part of Catholic worship.
For example: **Using holy water:** we make the sign of the cross with holy water when we enter a church to remind us of our baptism.

At Mass: You will learn about the people or things that you will see at Mass.
For example: **We stand when the Gospel is read. Why?** The four Gospels are the most precious part of the Bible. We stand out of respect for this word of God, ready to receive the Good News of Jesus Christ.

Bible: Indicates a Bible reading.

Special words: Words new to you will be explained. See the lists on p.44 and pp.134-135, and tick the relevant box when you come across the word.
For example: **Christian:** Christian is the name given to followers of Christ.

Search the church: In this box you will be asked to look around your church to find a particular item after Mass or when the church is quiet.
For example: **Cross:** a symbol of Christ for all Christians. How many crosses can you find in your church?

Journey candle: Look on the top corner of each page. You can colour your "journey" towards your First Holy Communion.

Chapter One

In the name of the Father

Introductory Rites

Every Sunday our parish family gathers together to celebrate the Mass or "Eucharist". **Draw a picture of your church.**

When I go to church I dip my fingers in holy water and **make the sign of the cross.**

Mass:
Also called the Eucharist – the celebration of the death and resurrection of Jesus. ✔ P.135

Eucharist:
Comes from a Greek word meaning "to give thanks". It is also used to mean the body and blood of Jesus. ✔ P.134

Celebrant:
The priest or bishop who leads us through the Mass.

Vestments:
Clothes that the priest and other sacred ministers wear when celebrating Mass and other services.

Everyday Life

I belong to the parish of:

St James

I meet some of my friends at church. I usually see:

peter

ella

If I had a pet DOG,
I would call it:

If I had a pet CAT,
I would call it:

The Lord says, "I can never forget you! I have written your name on the palms of my hands." (Isaiah 49:16)

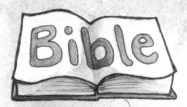

The Bible tells us about God. It tells us how to live as the people of God and as followers of his Son, Jesus. The Bible is like a guide, bringing us God's message.

The Old Testament

The Old Testament is the first part of the Bible.
It was written long before Jesus was born. Here is a story from the very beginning of the Old Testament. It is about Adam naming the animals.

God made out of the earth all the wild animals and all the birds of heaven. God brought them all to the man to see what he would call them. Whatever the man called each living creature, that was its name.

 (Genesis 2:19)

The Bible is often called the "Word of God". Can you think why?

People wanted to give **God a name**

God is a king

God is a judge

Jesus came to tell us God is a
loving parent

The New Testament

The New Testament is the second part of the Bible.
It has stories about Jesus in it.
In the New Testament we hear that Mary was going to have a
baby and she was to call him Jesus.

The angel said to Mary,
"You will bear a son,
and you will give
him the name Jesus.
He will be great and will
be called the Son of
the Most High."

 (Luke 1:31-32)

When Jesus grew up he was baptised in the River Jordan. He heard a voice from heaven saying,

"This is my beloved Son. I am delighted with him."

THE WHOLE STORY OF **THE BAPTISM OF JESUS**

John the Baptist was baptising people in the River Jordan. People used to be baptised in those days to show they were sorry for their sins. Jesus had never done anything wrong, but he waded out into the river and asked John to baptise him.

At first John didn't want to baptise him, but Jesus insisted.

Jesus went down under the water as if he were drowning, and then came up for breath.

All of a sudden something wonderful happened. The heavens opened, and the Spirit of God came to Jesus in the form of a dove.

Then Jesus heard a voice like thunder.

The voice said, **"This is my beloved Son. I am delighted with him."**

 (Adapted from Matthew 3:13-17)

6

Colour in this picture of Jesus being baptised in the River Jordan by John the Baptist.

Holy water:
Look for the holy water in the church.
Clue: it will be near the church doorway
or entrance. It is there to remind us of baptism: a
symbol of being washed clean.

7

Church

I was **baptised** at...

_____

Church. When I was baptised the priest said to me,

" _____ I baptise you in the name of the Father, and of the Son, and of the Holy Spirit."

When I was baptised God said to me,

" _____

you are my beloved child.
I am delighted with you. "

The sign of the cross
When I go to church I dip my finger in the holy water and say, **"In the name of the Father, and of the Son, and of the Holy Spirit."**

Baptism:
When I go to the Eucharist I will remember that my baptism links me up with everyone else in church. ✔ P.134

We are all beloved children of God – all equally loved by God. There is an extra-special bond of love between those who are baptised.

We pray to God, our loving parent.

Our Father, who art in heaven, hallowed be thy name; thy kingdom come, thy will be done on earth, as it is in heaven. Give us this day our daily bread, and forgive us our trespasses, as we forgive those who trespass against us; and lead us not into temptation, but deliver us from evil.

Everyday Life

The story of Adam tells us that God makes us all, and gives us this beautiful world to care for. Jesus shows us how to live as children of God.

I can **LIVE** like a beloved child of God, because I **AM** a beloved child of God. I have the Holy Spirit with me, just as Jesus did.

This week I am going to live like a child of God by...

Find all these words about God, our Father.

KIND   GENEROUS   PATIENT   WONDERFUL   CARING

LOVING   THOUGHTFUL   FUN

```
G E N E R O U S P T N E I T A P
N N U Z Y P L U F T H G U O H T
I I I G D O M F R I X K K I N D
V H E R P P S W R N A E I H G D
O D F W A G H A Y U K Y N D C V
L E H C N C C L U F R E D N O W
```

Family Time

Talk about **your** baptism and draw a picture of the baptismal font in your church.

_____

_____

_____

_____

The breeze of God's love is being carried around the world by the Holy Spirit.

Before you begin to pray,
quieten yourselves.

Lord God,
you know each one of us by
our own
special name;
you know all our families, you
love us so much.
Please help us to share your
love with everyone we meet.
We make this prayer through
Jesus your Son. Amen.

Baptismal font:
Look for the font where babies and
adults are baptised. It may look like a shallow
basin on a stand, or may be much larger.

Amen:
It is saying, "YES, I do believe." ✔ P.44

Chapter Two

Lord, have mercy

Penitential Act

Katie had a  for her **birthday**, but the kitten wouldn't go near her. **It hid under the** .
"Poor thing!" said Katie.
And she  **gave him a** . **"You're cold."** Still the kitten wouldn't go near her. "Poor thing!" said Katie.
"You're thirsty." And she gave him a
of . The little kitten still hid. Was Katie angry? OH NO! **"Poor thing!"** she said.
"You're hungry." And she gave him some .
And still the little kitten hid. **Katie** loved her little kitten. **"Poor thing!"** she said. **"You're very, very frightened."** She gently picked him up and stroked him until his little stopped beating wildly. **"I'm going to call you** vanessa **,"** she said.

12

If you had a kitten that wouldn't go near you, what would you do? **Would you still love it?**

Perhaps you have a pet that was naughty. Tell your friends what the pet did. **Do you still love your pet?**

Perhaps you are naughty sometimes. **Do the grown-ups around you still love you?**

Draw a picture showing that your family still loves you after you have been naughty.

The mercy of God: is like the child dealing with the kitten

Join in with the **"Lord, have mercy"** next time you go to Mass...

Penitential Act:

Priest: Lord, have mercy.
People: Lord, have mercy.
Priest: Christ, have mercy.
People: Christ, have mercy.
Priest: Lord, have mercy.
People: Lord, have mercy.

Penitential Act:
This is a form of words we use when we ask for forgiveness and healing for anything that separates us from each other and from God. When we do this with true honesty we receive God's forgiveness.

The Old Testament

Last session we talked about the wonderful world God made, and how wonderfully **WE** are made. But even so, there is a lot of unhappiness in the world. Here is a very old story, written before Jesus was born, that tries to explain why people can be full of hope, even though things seem to go wrong.

Adam and Eve lived in a beautiful garden where there were all sorts of wonderful fruit to eat. God said they could eat anything they liked, but there was one tree that they mustn't eat the fruit of, because if they did it would kill them.

Now the snake was the craftiest of all the creatures in the garden. He hated the man and woman. He slithered up to Eve and told her that if she ate this fruit she would live for ever.

Eve ate the fruit, and gave some to Adam. Straight away they were very frightened, and hid away from God. God was very sorry that the man and woman had harmed themselves. From now onwards people would always have to work hard, and suffer, and die. But God had a wonderful idea.

God promised that one day another woman would have a son, and he would **SAVE** the world from despair. From then on, people waited for this **SAVIOUR**. God kept reminding people about the great **PROMISE** until at last the **PROMISE** was kept.

We know the promise has been kept. The person who came to save us was

Jesus.

(Adapted from Genesis 3)

When Jesus grew up he told lots of stories to teach us about God. What does this one tell us about God?

The story of a forgiving father

There was once a father who had two sons. The younger son was fed up working for his father, and he asked if he could have his share of the money **NOW**. The father sadly gave his son the money.

Off went the son to a faraway country. He bought good clothes, he made lots of friends, and gave lots of parties. After a while he ran out of money and his friends left him. To make matters worse a terrible famine hit the country. The younger son was starving. He managed to get some

work, but it wasn't very nice. He had to look after some pigs. He was so hungry he wanted to eat the pig food, but no one offered him any.

At last the younger son came to his senses. **"Even my father's servants are better off than this,"** he said. **"I'll go back and say I'm sorry.**

"I'll say I'm not good enough to be his son, so please could I be his servant. Then I'll get some good food again." He trudged along, practising what he would say to his father. His father saw him coming while he was still a long way off, and ran out to meet him joyfully.

"Quick!" the father shouted to the servants. **"Get some fine clothes for my son. Get a ring for his finger and sandals for his feet. Kill the fatted calf and let's have a party. My son was lost but he is found. I thought he was dead but he's alive."**

Meanwhile the elder son was coming back from working in the fields. He was really hurt when he discovered what all the fuss was about.

"I've been working all hours for you," he grumbled, **"and you've never had a party for me. But now here comes your good-for-nothing son, and you kill the fatted calf. It's not fair."**

"My son, you know that all I have is yours," said the kind father. **"I love you both. But it is only right that we should celebrate now. For my son was lost but now he is found. He was dead, but now he is alive."**

 (Adapted from Luke 15:11-32)

Colour this picture of the forgiving father.

During the **"Lord, have mercy"** at Mass we are like the younger son who came to his senses. We realise that we make bad choices that hurt ourselves and others. We turn to God and ask God to forgive us for anything we want to say "sorry" for. For example, when:

- ♥ **we have been like Adam and got things wrong.**
- ♥ **we have been like the younger son thinking only of ourselves.**

Then we can say,

"Lord, have mercy."

God is like the loving father in the story – delighted to see us.

God is always full of love.

Mercy is a very special kind of love. Mercy is:

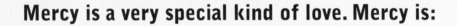

Kindness   Understanding   Forgiveness   Patience

God showed mercy to the very first human beings and promised a Saviour. The father showed mercy to the younger son and gave him a party. God our loving Father shows us mercy, and at the Eucharist God gives us special food. This food is Jesus the Saviour, the bread of life. He gives us the strength to live as the children of God.

- ♥ When we show mercy we become more God-like.
- ♥ Mercy is something that only those with power can give. It is more positive than just not punishing.

Everyday Life

Every time we show mercy, no matter how angry we feel inside, we are learning to be more like God who is always loving and merciful.

When I have been selfish I feel **bad**

Sorry

When I have hurt someone, I can say

Once I made up with

by

We can show mercy...

through patience at home by

through kindness at school by

19

Family Time

Write a prayer of your own, asking God for something for which you need help.

PRAYER TO SAY TOGETHER

Jesus,

I trust in your love and forgiveness.

I am sorry for all the wrong things

I have done. I am sorry for all the

good things that I have not done.

I want to love you with all my heart.

Amen.

WRITE YOUR PRAYER HERE

Find all these words about God our Father.

PATIENCE

MERCY **LOVE** **KINDNESS** **LORD** **FATHER**

R	P	D	K	M	E	R	C	Y	O	P	H	J	K	L	G
E	N	U	Z	Y	P	L	U	F	T	H	G	U	O	O	T
H	I	I	D	S	S	E	N	D	N	I	K	K	I	V	D
T	H	E	R	R	P	V	W	R	N	A	E	I	H	E	D
A	D	F	W	A	O	O	A	Y	U	K	Y	N	D	C	V
F	E	H	C	N	C	L	L	E	C	N	E	I	T	A	P

Chapter Three

Celebrating our rescue

Reconciliation

Becoming friends again

Use this page for your own drawing or design, or make up a collage of pictures from magazines or newspapers.

Reconciliation:
To bring together and be friends again.
✔ P.44

Here are some questions about difficult times you may have had in your life.

1. Have you ever rescued anything that you love very much?

2. Have you been in trouble or in danger before?

3. Have you ever seen anyone rescued from a fire or water or a road accident?

Was it very difficult?

How did you feel afterwards?

Tell everyone about it.

Child Found Safe on Mountain Ledge

PARENTS OVERJOYED

HIJACKED PLANE
HOSTAGES RELEASED

SAFE!

Draw a picture of something or someone being rescued.

People need to be rescued from accidents on the road, on the beach, at sea, from fires. Perhaps people need to be rescued from bullies or from getting lost. An animal may need rescuing. Ask your parents for some ideas.

The Old Testament

There are lots of "rescue" stories in the Old Testament. Here is one about Daniel rescued from the lions' den.

There was once a brave young man called Daniel. Some men were jealous of Daniel, but they couldn't get him into trouble because he was so good. The bad men thought of a trick.

They got the king to agree that anyone who prayed to God should be thrown into a pit of lions. The king agreed because he didn't know about the one true God.

Daniel went on praying to God, and the bad men told the king. The king was very sad. He knew Daniel was a good man, but he had to keep his word. He threw Daniel into the lions' den.

In the morning the king went to the lions' den. There he saw something wonderful. Daniel was alive. Daniel told the king that God had **RESCUED** him because he had trusted in God. After that the king believed in God. He told the whole world that Daniel's God was full of power. Daniel's God **SAVES** and **RESCUES**.

(Adapted from Daniel 6)

25

The New Testament

Jesus wanted to tell us how God is always ready to RESCUE us. He used stories to help us realise it. You have already heard the story of the forgiving father. When the younger brother came home the father rescued him from hunger and poverty. He even gave him a party, because he was so glad his son was found.

Here is another story Jesus told.

There was once a shepherd who had a hundred sheep. Every night he counted them carefully as he put them into the sheepfold. One evening when he counted, he noticed that one was missing. He knew who it was, as he knew them all by name. It was one of the little lambs.
He decided to go out and look for it because there was great danger on the hillside. It might fall down a cliff or be eaten by wild animals. Once he saw that the other sheep were safely in the fold, he set off to look for his lost lamb. It grew darker and darker, but still he kept on looking, and calling out for his lost lamb.

He heard the wild animals growling, and felt the wind growing stronger and stronger, but he would not give up hope. At last, near the edge of a cliff, he heard a frightened bleat. It was his lost lamb. Carefully, he climbed down to where the lamb had fallen, and RESCUED it. He gently put it over his shoulders and carried it back to the fold. Then the shepherd called his friends and neighbours. "Let's celebrate," he said, "for I have found my lost sheep."

(Adapted from Luke 15:4-7)

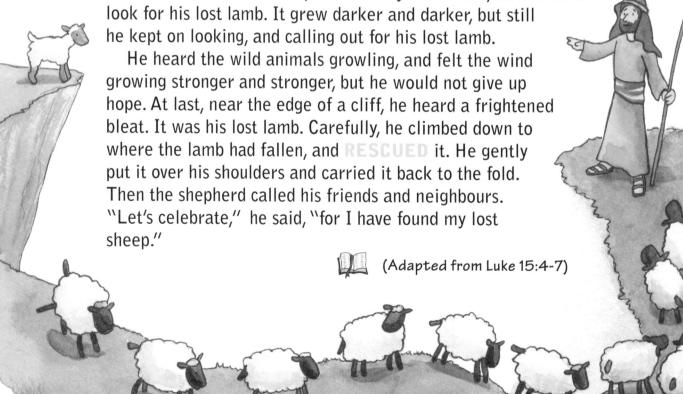

Colour this picture of the good shepherd finding his lost sheep.

Everyday Life

We are just like the people that heard the stories Jesus told. We are children of God, and we are full of love and joy and wonderful feelings. However, sometimes we have other feelings that are not very nice.

We might feel...

ANGRY SPITEFUL GREEDY JEALOUS CRAFTY

We have to work out which feelings are constructive (helpful) and which are destructive (unhelpful). For example, sometimes anger can be a constructive thing, but spitefulness can never be.

If I have destructive feelings I know I need someone to **RESCUE** me. I am like the lost sheep that couldn't **RESCUE** itself. Sometimes I feel really lost and helpless. My destructive feelings take me over. But God is my **RESCUER**. When I feel lost and helpless, God comes to my **RESCUE** and saves me.

Draw a picture here of you and your friend sorting things out with God's help.

When we have sorted it out we have been **reconciled**.

Reconciliation...

... is happening all the time in our lives. Every time we sort things out with our parents, teachers, and friends, we are being **RECONCILED**.

We go to **RECONCILIATION** to **CELEBRATE** all the times we forgive each other.

We go to **RECONCILIATION** to **CELEBRATE** all the times God forgives us.

Life is full of **RECONCILIATION**, so life is full of **CELEBRATION**.

When you go to **RECONCILIATION** in church you are **CELEBRATING** with all the people of God.

The priest is standing in for them. Most importantly, the priest is also standing in for God.

When you talk to the priest during **RECONCILIATION** it is **YOUR SPECIAL TIME**.

Nobody else will ever know what you are saying to him. What you say is between **YOU** and **GOD**.

You can say **ANYTHING** to the priest, because in **RECONCILIATION** you are really talking to God your loving **RESCUER**.

Reconciliation:
Brought back together again, we CELEBRATE God's love and ongoing help. ✔ P.44

The sacrament of reconciliation:
A sign and celebration which brings God's loving forgiveness. ✔ P.44

One of the things you could say is...

I have come to ask God to forgive me for

(and then say something you did or said that you know was deliberately unloving).

Reconciliation is about:
CELEBRATING our rescue in the past; GETTING HELP for the future.

In the sacrament of
RECONCILIATION God gives us hope
and strength for problems that still
aren't sorted out.

We promise that, with God's help, we
will be more loving in future.

**We will think more about this next time
we meet.**

A word search on rescue words

JOY RELIEF RESCUED STRENGTH SORRY
FORGIVENESS LOVE HELP CELEBRATION

```
F J K L O V E Y R W Q O O I A B
O I Z B E E F N M J F E I L E R
R S P L K M B G T W S Z T P X E
G Z T X C V B N M Y L K Y L H S
I M N R B X Z W Q O T P J E G C
V T R H E K L Y O J O Y L T Y U
E C V B N N Q H G O F P N R L E
N E E R R N G M K Y Y Y B W K D
E T G O N O I T A R B E L E C M
S K L P Y T F G H V B S W T U H
S O R R Y K L P H H A E I V C G
```

Are you lost with this word search?
Do you need **RESCUING?**
Ask someone to help!

31

Family Time

Reconciliation:

Find the place in the church where you will receive the sacrament of reconciliation.

Stations of the Cross:

A devotion practised particularly in Lent, recalling the journey that Jesus took on Good Friday from Pilate's court to Calvary. There are 14 stopping places where prayers are said. The pictures or sculptures are found on the walls of most Catholic churches.

Write a prayer thanking God for rescuing you when you did something unkind.

A THANK YOU PRAYER

Draw a picture of you doing some loving and kind things for other people.

Chapter Four

God helps me get it right

Reconciliation

People who have helped me get things right.

On this page you can write about people, draw people, or stick in pictures or photographs.

Everyday Life

Is there anything you wanted to do when you were younger, but it seemed too difficult?

Who helped you to get it right in the end?

The people you live with should care for you. If you are frightened of something, like learning to swim, or being in the class assembly, they should encourage you to have a go. When they trust you with things, like important messages, or keeping an eye on the baby, it helps you believe in yourself, because they believed in you first.

Here I am being helped by someone to GET IT RIGHT

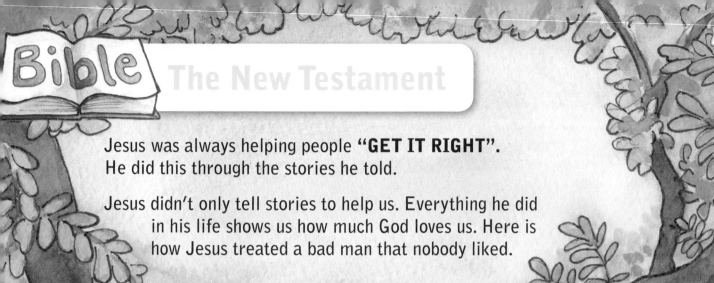
Jesus was always helping people **"GET IT RIGHT"**. He did this through the stories he told.

Jesus didn't only tell stories to help us. Everything he did in his life shows us how much God loves us. Here is how Jesus treated a bad man that nobody liked.

ZACCHAEUS – THE MAN JESUS BELIEVED IN

Zacchaeus was a mean, greedy man. He had hardly any friends because all he cared about was money. One day he heard Jesus was coming to town. He was very curious about him, and decided to go along and see him.

Zacchaeus was very short and there were lots of people crowding around. They wouldn't let Zacchaeus get to the front. Jesus was coming nearer, and Zacchaeus gave up all hope of seeing him.

Suddenly he had an idea. There was a sycamore tree nearby. He decided he would climb the tree. He didn't care if the people laughed at him. He would have a really good view of Jesus.

Imagine his surprise when Jesus stopped beneath the tree! Jesus looked up at him and smiled.

"Come down, Zacchaeus," said Jesus. **"I'd really love to have a meal with you today."**

Zacchaeus was thrilled to hear such good news. He knew he had treated people badly by cheating them out of their money. That was why he had hardly any friends.

It was amazing that Jesus actually wanted to come to his house.

As Jesus and Zacchaeus chatted, something strange happened. Money didn't seem so important to Zacchaeus any more. It was much more fun talking to Jesus. Zacchaeus began to realise how lonely he had been. He felt sorry about what he had been like in the past, but he knew that he had changed. Jesus cared for him, and that made all the difference. **"I know what I'll do,"** he told Jesus. **"I'll give half my money away to the people who really need it, and if I've cheated anyone, I'll give them back four times as much as I took from them."**

(Adapted from Luke 19:1-10)

In what way did Zacchaeus change?

Why did he decide to be generous to his neighbours?

38

Colour this picture of Jesus helping Zacchaeus to "GET IT RIGHT".

Conscience:
God has given us the power to tell us whether an act is right or wrong before we do it. ✔ P.44

Sin: Freely choosing to do something which we know is wrong ✔ P.44

We can tell the priest anything we are worried about, or that we would like to put right. The priest is there to show us Jesus' understanding and love.

Contrition: Being sorry for doing wrong. ✔ P.44

Act of Sorrow or Contrition
O my God,
I am sorry for what I have done wrong,
I know you love me and I want to love you too.
With your help I will try not to sin again.
Amen.

We go to reconciliation for God's help. God can help us put things right.

Remember that what you say is a secret between you and Jesus. The priest can't tell anyone what you tell him, because he is only standing in for Jesus.

Jesus is with us in a special way in the sacrament of reconciliation, just as he and Zacchaeus were together long ago.

We can't see Jesus now, so the priest takes his place.
Zacchaeus loved talking to Jesus. He told him all the things he couldn't tell anyone else, because he knew Jesus would understand.

We can talk to Jesus too.

You could write your own sorry prayer in the space below and say it with your night prayers when you go to bed.

Here is a picture of me saying that with God's help I will be more loving in future. You can draw yourself sitting or kneeling at reconciliation.

41

The sacrament of reconciliation
Examination of conscience

Before the sacrament

Think back over the good times and the bad times you have had lately. Thank God for the good times. Even the bad times probably had some good bits. For instance, it is good to make up with someone we have had a row with.
We can go to reconciliation to **CELEBRATE** these good bits.
Sometimes we haven't been able to put the bad things right.
We can go to reconciliation to get help for these things.
Talk to God in your heart about these things.

During the sacrament

Tell the priest how long it is since you last went.
(You can't do this at your first reconciliation!)
Tell him what you want to tell Jesus – the things you need help with.
LISTEN to what the priest says to you. He will ask you to say a little prayer or do something kind during the week, to show your love of God and of everyone else.
LISTEN CAREFULLY to the wonderful words of forgiveness he says.
We know God always forgives us,
but it is good to hear it put into words.

Absolve:
To set free
from. ✔ P.44

After the sacrament

Thank God for the chance to celebrate reconciliation. If the priest asked you to say a prayer, say it straight away before you forget. This is called your **PENANCE**.
Say a prayer for the priest.

Penance:
Something we
do to show
we are sorry for doing
wrong. ✔ P.44

Find the names in the word search of these people whom God helped to get it right. Then look up their stories in the Bible.

PETER   **ZACCHAEUS**   **PAUL**

MARY MAGDALENE   **THE GOOD THIEF**

```
F P L E N E L A D G A M Y R A M
T H E G O O D T H I E F I L E R
R S P L K M B G T W S Z T P X E
G Z T X C V B N M Y L K Y L H T
I M N R B X Z W Q O T P J E G E
V T S U E A H C C A Z Y L U A P
```

Look up stories in the Bible using the following references:

PETER	Luke, chapter 22: verses 54-62	(Luke 22:54-62)
LOST COIN	Luke, chapter 15: verses 8-10	(Luke 15:8-10)
GOOD THIEF	Luke, chapter 23: verses 39-43	(Luke 23:39-43)
PRODIGAL SON	Luke, chapter 15: verses 11-32	(Luke 15:11-32)
LOST SHEEP	Luke, chapter 15: verses 4-7	(Luke 15:4-7)

Bible: A library of holy books, bound togther in one volume, through which God tells people about God and God's love for them. ✔ P.44

43

Family Time

You have celebrated the **sacrament of reconciliation**. Talk about these special words from the reconciliation chapters.

Absolve: To set free from.

Amen: It is saying, "Yes, I do believe."

Bible: A library of holy books, bound together in one volume, through which God tells people about God and God's love for them.

Christian: Christian is the name given to followers of Christ.

Conscience: A God-given power within us, which tells us whether an act is right or wrong before we do it.

Contrition: Being sorry for doing wrong.

Penance: Something we do to show we are sorry for doing wrong.

Reconciliation: To bring together and be friends again.

Sin: Freely choosing to do something which we know is wrong.

The sacrament of reconciliation: A sign and celebration which brings God's loving forgiveness.

Chapter Five

Glory to God in the highest

Glory to God

Joy!

Hallelujah

Praise

Here are two special experiences that might happen to you one day.

Which one do you prefer?

fireworks

Andrew felt his heart pounding as he raced for the ball. He reached it just before his opponent, and kicked it with all his might. **"Yes!"** shouted Andrew. **"GOAL!"** roared the crowd. In the last minute of play Andrew had scored. **His team had won the cup!**

The firework display was the best Sarah had ever been to. Rockets zoomed into the sky and showered silver stars above the trees. Catherine-wheels whizzed round and round, and golden fountains rained sparkling jewels everywhere.

Draw a picture of a special experience that you have had which made you want to praise and thank God.

It may be a picture of our beautiful world of nature, a beach, the crashing of waves, a sunset, a baby, your friends, an animal, the work of an insect, music, sport; it is your choice.

All special experiences are gifts from God. Sometimes they are wild and exciting. Sometimes they are peaceful and dreamy. Sometimes the most ordinary things seem somehow different and glorious. All these experiences come from God who makes everything.

They all show the GLORY OF GOD.

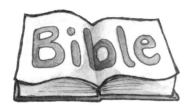

The Old Testament

In the **Old Testament** there are people who had very special experiences of God. They could see the GLORY OF GOD.

Moses is one of these people. (You might know the story of when he was a baby and his mother hid him in the river to save his life. Ask someone to tell you the story if you don't know it.) Here is the story of a very important experience of the glory of God that Moses had.

Moses used to look after his father-in-law's sheep. One day he led the flock right into the middle of the desert until he came to the great Mount Horeb. All of a sudden he saw something very strange.

There was a GLORIOUS bush nearby that was blazing with light.

The bush was on fire! What was so strange about it was that although the bush was burning brightly, it was not being burnt up. It just blazed and blazed with the most GLORIOUS light. Moses wondered what he should do. The burning bush was so strange it was frightening, but it was so beautiful he wanted to go nearer. As soon as he plucked up courage to go nearer he heard a voice calling him.

"Moses! Moses!"
"Here I am!" said Moses.
The voice said, **"Do not come any closer, and take off your sandals. You are standing on HOLY GROUND."**
The voice went on to say,
"I am the God of your father, the God of Abraham, the God of Isaac, the God of Jacob."
Moses hid his face, for he didn't dare look into the face of God. God told Moses to save God's people from the wicked Pharaoh. Moses was to be their SAVIOUR, and lead them out of slavery, and into freedom, to a Promised Land. In this land there would be food and drink for everyone. It would be flowing with milk and honey!

 (Adapted from Exodus 3:1-10)

The New Testament

For hundreds of years people waited for God to send a Saviour. WE know that God's glorious plan was to become a human being, but in those days nobody knew. They just waited and waited.

They waited for a GLORIOUS King   KNGI

They waited for a GLORIOUS leader   LEDREA

They waited to see the glory of God in powerful and mighty signs.
Mary waited for a tiny baby. She knew that the glory of God would be hidden in her little son.

You know the story of how God kept the GLORIOUS promise. Jesus was born in a stable at Bethlehem. **Here is the story of how some shepherds were the first to hear the GOOD NEWS – the quiet glory of Jesus' birth.**

Just outside Bethlehem there were some shepherds up in the hilltops. They were guarding their sheep from the wolves and other wild creatures, but it was a peaceful sort of night with nothing much happening.

All of a sudden an angel of the Lord stood by them, and the glory of God shone round about them. They were very, very frightened. But the angel said to them,

**"Do not be afraid. I have some great news for you, and for everybody. For today in Bethlehem a SAVIOUR is born, who is CHRIST THE LORD. And this shall be a sign for you.
You will find the baby wrapped in swaddling clothes and lying in a manger."**

And suddenly there was a whole crowd of angels GLORIFYING God and singing,

"GLORY TO GOD IN THE HIGHEST AND PEACE TO GOD'S PEOPLE ON EARTH."

After the shepherds had seen the baby they went away glorifying and praising God and telling everyone they met what had happened.

(Adapted from Luke 2:8-20)

The shepherds saw the GLORY of GOD on the hillside and the GLORY of GOD in the manger. **What was the same about each kind of glory? What was different?**

Church

When we go to church for the Eucharist we are like the shepherds seeing the glory of God. Sometimes we can experience the glory. Usually it is hidden. Sometimes we have a chance to sing the song of glory and praise the angels sang.

Glory to God in the highest, and on earth peace to people of good will.
We praise you, we bless you, we adore you, we glorify you,
we give you thanks for your great glory,
Lord God, heavenly King, O God, almighty Father.
Lord Jesus Christ, Only Begotten Son,
Lord God, Lamb of God, Son of the Father,
you take away the sins of the world,
have mercy on us;
you take away the sins of the world,
receive our prayer;
you are seated at the right hand of the Father,
have mercy on us.
For you alone are the Holy One,
you alone are the Lord,
you alone are the Most High,
Jesus Christ, with the Holy Spirit,
in the glory of God the Father.
Amen.

Glory to God

JOY!

Hallelujah

Praise

A	H	O	S	A	N	N	A	K
X	P	R	A	I	S	E	L	H
N	S	X	Y	R	O	L	G	J
U	U	S	K	N	A	H	T	R
Y	P	G	R	E	A	T	M	S
D	E	H	O	N	O	U	R	O
G	R	X	E	R	O	D	A	A

GLORY
PRAISE
SUPER
HOSANNA
ADORE
GREAT
THANKS
HONOUR

The glory of God was seen most powerfully in Jesus, but the glory of God is also shining in each one of us.
Draw a picture showing how God is sharing God's glory with you.

Family Time

 In church, listen out for how many times the word "**GLORY**" and similar words are mentioned.

Today we counted _____ **times!**

To talk about at home.
When the shepherds left the magnificent glory of God on the hillside, they arrived at the quiet glory of a baby in a manger. At Mass we meet the quiet glory of God under the appearance of bread and wine.

In this chapter you have been thinking about the "**GLORIA**", but there are other important prayers of praise.

Look at a Preface in a Mass book; it is full of thanks and praise.
The priest ends the Eucharistic Prayer with the words: "Through him, and with him, and in him, O God, almighty Father, in the unity of the Holy Spirit, all glory and honour is yours, for ever and ever."

Palm Sunday:

The Sunday before Easter Sunday. Christians all over the world remember the day that Jesus rode into Jerusalem. The crowd shouted: "Hosanna to the Son of David!" There is often a parade or procession into church with singing and prayers. Listen for the word "hosanna" during the Mass.

Dear God,
we thank you for the sudden glory of a rainbow.
We thank you for the quiet glory of the stars.
We thank you for the magnificent glory of fireworks.
We thank you for

....

....

....
(what would you like to say?)

We thank you for the wonderful glory of Jesus being born.
We thank you especially for your glorious love,
which you showed by sending Jesus to be our Saviour.

We can end all our prayers with the "Glory be to the Father".
Glory be to the Father and to the Son and to the Holy Spirit.
As it was in the beginning, is now, and ever shall be, world without end. Amen.

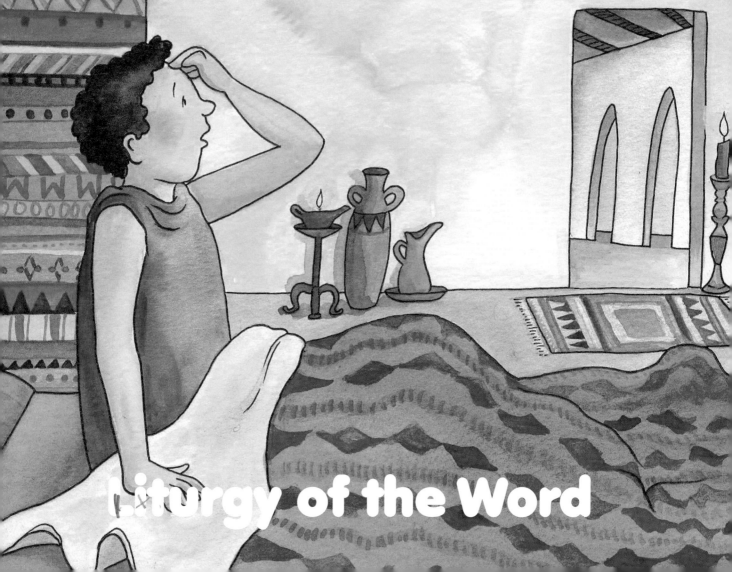

The word of the Lord

Liturgy of the Word

Choose a favourite story from the Bible and draw it, or write about it, saying what you like about it.

 Liturgy:
The worship of God in public prayer. ✔ P.135

 Parable:
A story with a message. Jesus often told stories to help people understand his message.

Liturgy of the Word: The part of the Mass when we listen to God's word – to readings from the Bible.

 Find a Bible or book of Bible stories at home, or at school, or in the library.

 Ask someone who cares for you what their favourite Bible story is, and why.

Everyday Life

What is missing from these animals? **Draw in what is missing.** Think about how well these animals would survive without them.

57

```
C  R  A  C  K  L  E
M  P  K  J  X  B  L
I  I  L  A  U  H  Z
A  N  K  Z  G  Q  Z
O  G  Z  P  O  P  I
W  H  O  O  S  H  F
```

MIAOW
BUZZ
CRACKLE
FIZZLE
POP
PING
WHOOSH

How well would you survive if you didn't listen to the people who care for you?

Circle your answer »

Tell the group about a time you were glad you listened.

EASILY

WITH DIFFICULTY

NOT AT ALL

The Old Testament

Last time we talked about wonderful things. Sometimes they were grand and showy. Other times they were quiet and hidden. Here is a wonderful story about a young boy listening to God in the quiet of the night.

Samuel was a very special child. His mother, Hannah, had prayed to God for a baby for years. She promised God that if she had a baby, she would let him serve God in Israel's holiest shrine when he was old enough. God heard Hannah's prayers, and eventually Samuel was born.

When Samuel was still a young boy he went to live and
work in the holy shrine.
He helped the old priest Eli, who was going blind.
One night when it was very quiet he heard a voice
calling him. He thought it was Eli, so he jumped up
and ran to him.
"I didn't call you," said Eli.
"Go back to bed."
Samuel went back to bed, but he heard the
voice calling him again.
He jumped up and ran to Eli.

"Here I am. I HEARD you call me," said Samuel.

"I didn't call you," said Eli. "Go back to bed."

Samuel went back to bed, very puzzled.

He was just falling asleep when he **heard** the voice
call him for the third time. Up he jumped and ran to Eli.

"You did call me," he said. "I HEARD you."

This time Eli realised that it was God calling Samuel.

"Go back to bed," he said.

"If you **hear** the voice again, say,
'Speak, Lord, for your servant is listening'."

Samuel lay down and listened in the silence.

It was a very special time.

Once again God called Samuel:

"Samuel! Samuel!"

Full of wonder, Samuel said,

"Speak, Lord, for your servant is **listening**."

God gave Samuel a message for Eli.

It was the first message that Samuel heard from God.

When he grew up he often heard messages from God, and he
passed them on to anyone who would listen.

 (Adapted from 1 Samuel 3)

Messages from God?
We hear God's word and pass it on to others by talking about it.
Our baptism gave us the power to become "prophets".

60

The New Testament

At last, the time came for Jesus to be born. (Do you remember that the New Testament is all about Jesus?)

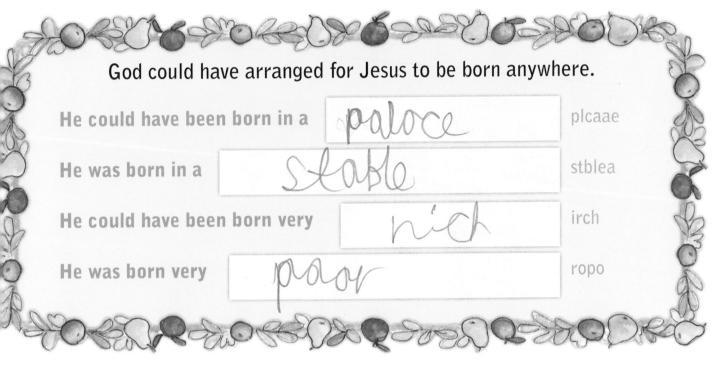

God could have arranged for Jesus to be born anywhere.

He could have been born in a	paloce	plcaae
He was born in a	stable	stblea
He could have been born very	rich	irch
He was born very	paor	ropo

He could have been born in splendour and loud glory. He was born in the quiet glory of the night.

JESUS IS THE WORD OF GOD

**At Christmas God's promise was kept.
JESUS was born in a quiet stable in Bethlehem.
JESUS is the Word of God.**

Signing with three crosses before the Gospel is read: This action reminds us to think about (cross on forehead), speak about (cross on lips), and love the Gospel (cross on heart).

Colour this picture of the WORD OF GOD born in a stable.

Church

Two thousand years ago, the **WORD OF GOD** lived with us as a human being. People could listen to Jesus as he spoke. Jesus is still with us today in many different ways. One of the ways he is with us is in the readings at Mass. When we listen to them we are listening to the **WORD OF GOD**.

The first reading is usually from the Old Testament. We hear about the times when people were still waiting for the Saviour.

At the end we hear the reader say:

"The word of the Lord."

We, in the congregation, respond:

"Thanks be to God."

The responsorial psalm, nearly always from the Old Testament, is a hymn of praise and is often used as our reply to God speaking to us. Jesus loved to sing these psalms.

The second reading is often from a letter listened to by the early Christians.

At the end we hear the reader say:

"The word of the Lord."

We, in the congregation, respond:

"Thanks be to God."

In the Gospel, we hear stories about the life of Jesus.

At the end we hear the priest or deacon say:

"The Gospel of the Lord." We, in the congregation, respond:

"Praise to you, Lord Jesus Christ." The Gospels written by M_a_t_t_h_e_n_, M A R K, L _u_ k _e_ and J _o_h_n_ contain the words of Jesus.

Here is a game for you to play. When you play it with your catechist you can all move when the catechist throws the dice. When you play it at home everyone can take turns at throwing the dice. I wonder if the best listener will always win!

START

Hear birds singing MOVE ON 2

Hear a good idea MOVE ON 5

Hear a favourite tune MOVE ON 2

STOP Didn't Listen MISS A TURN

Listen to a bad idea MOVE BACK 4

64

65

 **Family Time**

Say this family prayer together.

Open my eyes

Give me your strength

Lord, may I listen carefully to your words so that I can hear them.
Lord, may my heart be ready for your words so that I can love them.
Lord, may I be alert with open eyes so that I can see you in people.
Lord, make me strong and brave to do what your words tell me to do.
Here I am, Lord, speak to me.
Amen.

Open my heart

Open my ears

Write a prayer thanking God for things you like listening to.

_____

_____

_____

_____

 The Creed:
"Creed" means "I believe". The Creed is said all together after the priest has explained the Bible readings in his homily.

Lectern:
The reading desk from which the word of God is read.

Chapter Seven

Bread to offer

Liturgy of the Eucharist

Everyday Life

Once there was a little 🌰.
The ☀ shone and made it
GROW. It grew into a fine
wheat plant with hundreds of .
The  came and cut down the wheat.
She took it to the
to be ground into .
The **flour** was taken to the  to be
baked into .

A **BIG**  took it to the .

Someone bought the bread and took it home for the . They made sandwiches and had a great time!

68

Who gets the food in your house?

Who prepares it?

Do you help?

Draw you preparing a meal with people you like. It might be a picnic, or a birthday party, or just a meal you had when everyone was really hungry.

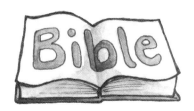

The Old Testament

Do you remember a while ago we were talking about Moses? He saw the glory of God in a burning bush, and God told him to save the Israelites from the wicked Pharaoh who was using them as slaves. Moses listened to God and led the slaves out of Egypt.

Moses and his people wandered in the desert for forty years, waiting for God to lead them into the Promised Land.

At first the people knew very little about God. They had to learn to trust God and to love one another. They had to learn that they were the people of God.

Here is the story of how God fed the people, and how they learnt to trust in God.

Out in the hot desert there was no food to eat. Everyone began to grumble to Moses.

"What's the point of bringing us out into the desert if we are going to die of starvation?" they said.

"We were better off as slaves. At least we had food to eat in Egypt."

God listened to their complaints and said to Moses, "I will let bread rain down from heaven. Then everyone can get what they need each day."

Moses told the people what God had said. When everyone woke in the morning, the ground was covered with something white, like frost.

"Man hu?" they all said. ("What's this?")

"This is the bread which God is giving you to eat," said Moses.

"Just collect as much as you need for today. There will be more tomorrow."

They were able to collect as much as they needed every day. They learnt to trust God and became a more organised group, rather than a rabble of escaped slaves. For their forty years in the desert, the people were given their daily bread. In which prayer do we ask for our daily bread?

 (Adapted from Exodus 16)

The New Testament

MOSES WAS A SAVIOUR **of his people, but Jesus is much greater than Moses.** JESUS IS THE SAVIOUR OF THE WORLD.

People loved to hear Jesus talk about God, and often they followed him out into the desert to listen to him.

Jesus was able to feed the people when they were hungry, just as Moses did.

Here is the story of the
FEEDING OF THE FIVE THOUSAND.

Great crowds used to follow Jesus because of all the people he cured. One day Jesus took a boat to a desert place, because he wanted to be alone for a while, but the people guessed where he was going and followed him there on foot. Jesus was sorry for everyone, and spent the whole day teaching them and healing the sick.

When evening came the crowds were really hungry, but there was nowhere to buy food in the desert.

Jesus' friends said, **"Send the people away, so they can get some food."**

Jesus said, **"There is no need to send them away. YOU feed them."**

The only person with any food on him was a young boy. His mother had packed a little picnic for him.

He had five small loaves of bread and two fish. The boy offered his food to the friends of Jesus. The friends took the boy to Jesus and showed him the loaves and fishes. **"Here is a boy with five loaves and two fish,"** they said, **"but that's not enough for all this crowd."** Jesus said, **"Make the people sit down in groups."**

When everyone sat down there were over five thousand people. Jesus took the loaves, gave thanks, and gave them out to the people. He did the same with the fish.

Everyone had as much as they wanted. When the scraps were gathered up, there were twelve baskets of food left over.

 (Adapted from John 6:1-13)

Colour this picture of the boy offering his food to be shared with the crowd.

Jesus turned the offering into something amazing. At Mass, we offer bread, wine, money, and our little sacrifices and triumphs of the week, and they are transformed into something wonderful.

73

Church

The first half of the Eucharist is called the
Liturgy of the Word.
Now we are going to think about the second half of the Eucharist. This is called the
Liturgy of the Eucharist.
At the beginning of the Liturgy of the Eucharist, everything has to be prepared, just like at home before you eat. Watch how the altar servers help the priest.

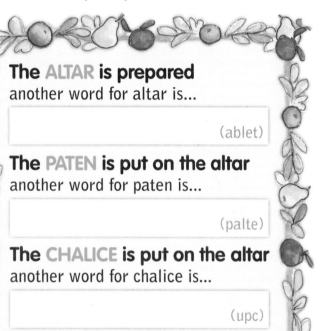

The ALTAR is prepared
another word for altar is...

_____

(ablet)

The PATEN is put on the altar
another word for paten is...

_____

(palte)

The CHALICE is put on the altar
another word for chalice is...

_____

(upc)

THE OFFERTORY PROCESSION

People bring gifts of bread and wine in procession to be put on the altar. They also bring gifts of money earned by the work of their hands. The priest then places the bread and wine on the altar while saying prayers to God, the Lord of all creation.

We remember that the bread and wine – all of creation – come from God.

We also remember that people work hard in God's creation so that we have food and drink. If people didn't work together and look after the world there would be no food. We thank God for all we have. We offer our thanks and say, **"BLESSED BE GOD FOR EVER."**

GIFTS OF BREAD AND WINE AND THE GIFT OF OURSELVES

We know Jesus used bread and wine at the Last Supper; that is why we use them. But there is also another meaning to them.

The bread is like all the everyday things we do: our daily routines, our daily effort, the ways in which we try to help others.

The wine is like all the excitement and special occasions: our laughter, our fun, our adventures, our hobbies, the good things we enjoy.
We are bringing all the parts of our life and placing them on the altar.

They are changed into the **body and blood of Jesus** and become an offering of Jesus himself. Together with himself, Jesus offers all of us – our thanksgiving, our praise, our sorrow – to the Father.

Altar:
The table of the Lord; the table for the sacrifice of the Mass.

Sacrifice:
Means "to offer". During the Mass, the priest, in the name of the people, makes present again Christ's offering of himself to the Father. We recognise that Jesus is Lord and Saviour and that we believe in him. ✔ P.135

75

Everyday Life

You may like to **write a prayer and draw a picture** for those less fortunate than yourself or **describe what you do or could do, in school,** as a fundraising event.

Draw:

Write:

_____

_____

_____

_____

_____

_____

Here is a word search. Find these words.

ALTAR **PATEN** **WINE** **OFFER** **DRINK**

CHALICE **BREAD** **FOOD** **THANKS**

```
Q A L T A R L A D O A M Y R A F
R F E H C O D T H P E F I L O R
E E F A L E C I L A H C T O X E
F W I N E V B K N T R D D L H T
F M N K R X Z W Q E T P J E G E
O T S S D R I N K N Z D A E R B
```

Holy, Holy, Holy Lord:
A great prayer of praise that we sing during the Eucharistic Prayer. It includes the word "hosanna", used by our ancestors when Jesus rode into Jerusalem, showing how much they loved and supported him.

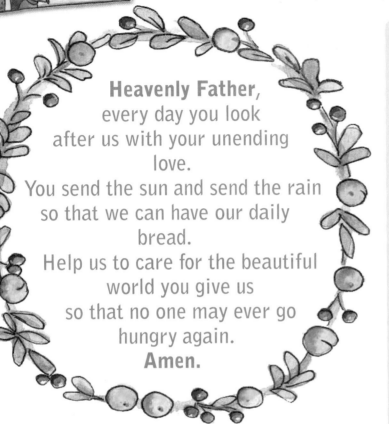

Family Time

Have a go at making bread: there are many different breads from around the world; the recipe below is from Ireland.

Heavenly Father,
every day you look
after us with your unending
love.
You send the sun and send the rain
so that we can have our daily
bread.
Help us to care for the beautiful
world you give us
so that no one may ever go
hungry again.
Amen.

Grace
before meals

Thank you, Lord, for this food and for the work of those who prepared it. Bless us as we share your gifts. **Amen.**

IRISH SODA BREAD

In a large bowl place:
200g self-raising wholemeal flour, 100g plain flour, ½ tsp. salt, 1 tsp. bicarbonate of soda, 15g brown sugar.
In a jug: beat together 200ml milk + 1 small egg.

Add most of the liquid to the flour bowl. Stir lightly with a knife, adding more milk if necessary to make soft, not sticky, dough. Knead lightly on a floured table until smooth, but only for 1 minute.
Shape into a round loaf 15cm in diameter.
Place on a baking sheet. Cut a cross on top of the bread.
Bake: 200°C Time: 20-30 minutes or until brown and sounds hollow when tapped on the bottom. Cool on a rack covered with a clean tea towel.
Eat within 1-2 days with your family.

Chapter Eight
Fruit of the vine

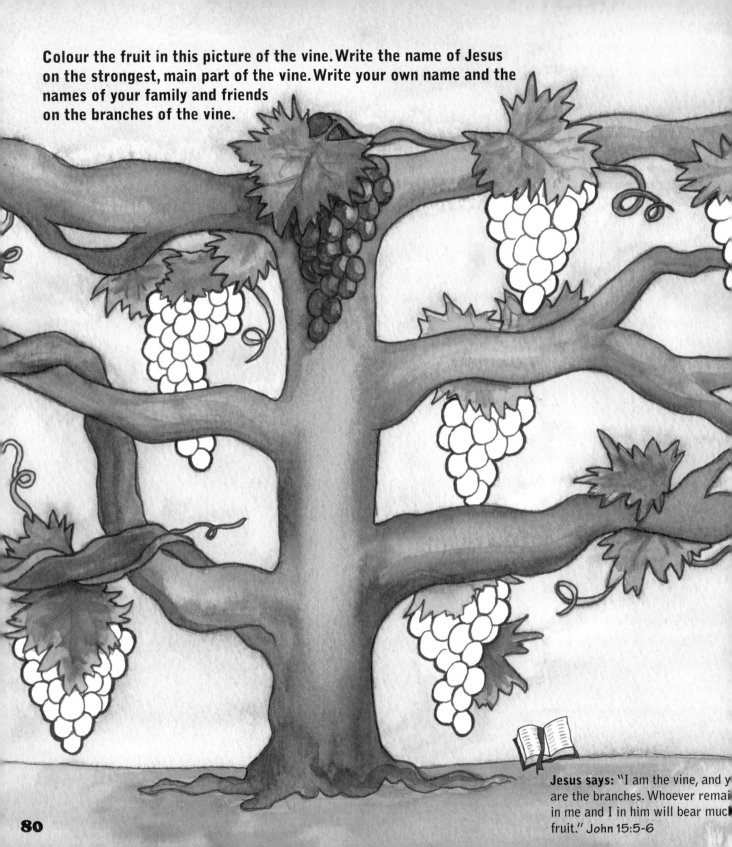

Colour the fruit in this picture of the vine. Write the name of Jesus on the strongest, main part of the vine. Write your own name and the names of your family and friends on the branches of the vine.

Jesus says: "I am the vine, and y͏͏ are the branches. Whoever remai in me and I in him will bear muc͏ fruit." John 15:5-6

80

Everyday Life

Have you been to a party recently?
What did you have to drink there?

• Put a tick next to the drinks you had at the party.
• Colour in all the drinks that grown-ups might have at a party.

Lemon

VIN ROUGE

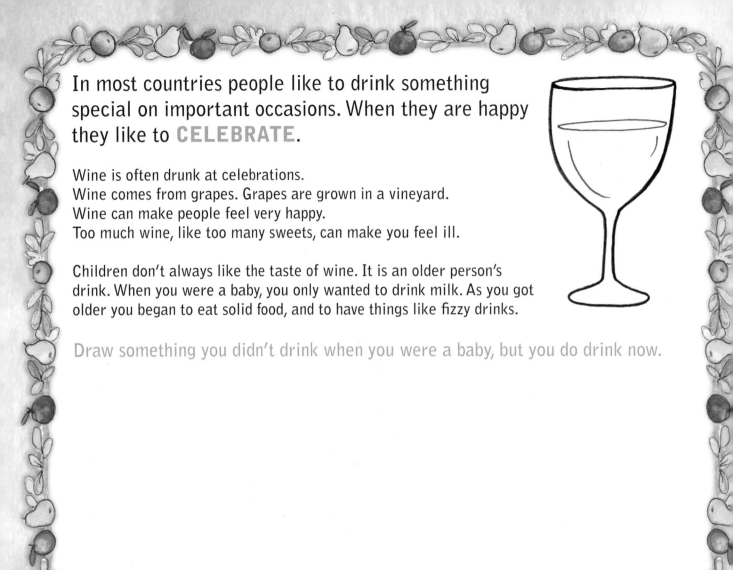

In most countries people like to drink something special on important occasions. When they are happy they like to **CELEBRATE**.

Wine is often drunk at celebrations.
Wine comes from grapes. Grapes are grown in a vineyard.
Wine can make people feel very happy.
Too much wine, like too many sweets, can make you feel ill.

Children don't always like the taste of wine. It is an older person's drink. When you were a baby, you only wanted to drink milk. As you got older you began to eat solid food, and to have things like fizzy drinks.

Draw something you didn't drink when you were a baby, but you do drink now.

Chalice:
The cup for the wine used at Mass.

The Old Testament

Eventually the people of God got to the Promised Land, and settled down. Every year they had several feasts which Jews still celebrate today.

The most important feast is the Passover, when they remember how God had saved them from slavery. At this feast four cups of wine are drunk. **The leader of the feast says this prayer before each cup of wine is drunk:**

"Blessed are you, O Lord our God,
King of the Universe,
Creator of the fruit of the vine."

Where have you heard a prayer like this before?

Wine was such a special drink that in the Bible the people of God are called the vineyard of God. (Remember, wine comes from grapes which grow in a vineyard.) Here is a song that Isaiah sang when the people didn't listen to the word of God.

My friend had a vineyard on a very rich hill.
He dug the soil and cleared it of stones.
He planted the finest vines.
He built a tower to guard them,
dug a pit for treading the grapes.
He waited for the grapes to ripen,
but every grape was sour.

(Isaiah 5:1-2)

Later on, Isaiah wrote this:

The Lord will say this of his pleasant vineyard.

"I watch over it and water it all the time. I guard it night and day so that no one will harm it... In days to come the people of Israel will take root like a tree, and they will bud. The earth will be covered with the fruit they produce."

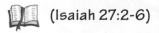 (Isaiah 27:2-6)

The New Testament

**Jesus loved to celebrate all the Jewish feasts.
He celebrated the sabbath every week.
He celebrated all the great yearly festivals.
He also celebrated with his friends when they got married.**

Weddings were very special celebrations for the Jews. They were special for the people getting married, and they were special because the love between a man and a woman was like the love between God and the people of God.
Here is the story of the first miracle Jesus did.

One day there was a wedding in the town of Cana. Mary was invited, and so were Jesus and his friends. Everyone was having a great time, but then they ran out of wine.

Mary noticed, so she went to Jesus and said, **"They have no wine left."** Jesus said that it was nothing to do with him as his time hadn't come yet. Mary went to the servants and said, **"Do whatever Jesus tells you to."**

The Jews had lots of very strict religious rules about washing, and there were six enormous water jars standing nearby. Jesus went to the servants and said, **"Fill these jars with water."** The servants did what Jesus said, filling them up to the brim.

Jesus said, **"Take some of the water out and give it to the head waiter to try."** The servants did this, and the head waiter tasted the water. It wasn't water any more! It had all changed into wine!

The head waiter didn't realise where all the wine had come from. He went to the man getting married and said to him, **"Most people serve the best wine first, and when everyone has had plenty to drink they bring out the ordinary wine. You have kept the best wine till now."**

This was the first sign that Jesus did. His friends saw how wonderful he was, and believed in him.

(Adapted from John 2:1-11)

How do you think the bride and groom felt when they ran out of wine? What difference did Jesus make to the wedding feast?

Colour this picture of the wedding feast at Cana.

When we go to the Eucharist there is so much to think about.

We can think about the PAST.

We can remember that the people of God were, and are, like a beautiful vineyard to God. We are also part of the people of God. We can remember how God delivers us from evil by sending us Jesus. We can be thankful for this.

Moses saved the original people of God. Jesus saves the whole world.

We can think about NOW.

Jesus makes all the difference to our lives. Jesus makes our lives a celebration. Because of him, we are also part of the vineyard of God.

Jesus said he was the vine and we are the branches. He is not separate from us: the vine IS the branches and the roots, and fruit!
"Whatever you do to the least one of these, you do it to me," said Jesus.

When we are at the Eucharist we can think of everyone we know and love. We can remember that we are all joined together by love. The love of Jesus makes us all one, just as all the branches of a vine make up one plant. When we drink from the chalice at the Eucharist we can be thankful for all the good things of life, especially love and friendship.

At the Eucharist we can also think about the FUTURE.

Jesus often spoke about heaven as an **EVERLASTING PARTY**.
When we receive Communion we can remember that one day there will be no more sin and sorrow. We shall see God face to face, and rejoice with God and the whole people of God for ever and ever.

This is what that beautiful new world will be like.

Then I saw a new heaven and a new earth. I saw the holy city, the new Jerusalem, coming down out of heaven from God, dressed like a bride ready to meet her husband. I heard a loud voice speaking from the throne: **"Now God's home is with people. He will live with them, and they shall be his people. God himself will be with them, and they shall be his people. He will wipe away all tears from their eyes. There will be no more death, no more grief or crying or pain. The old things have disappeared."**

(Revelation 21:1-4)

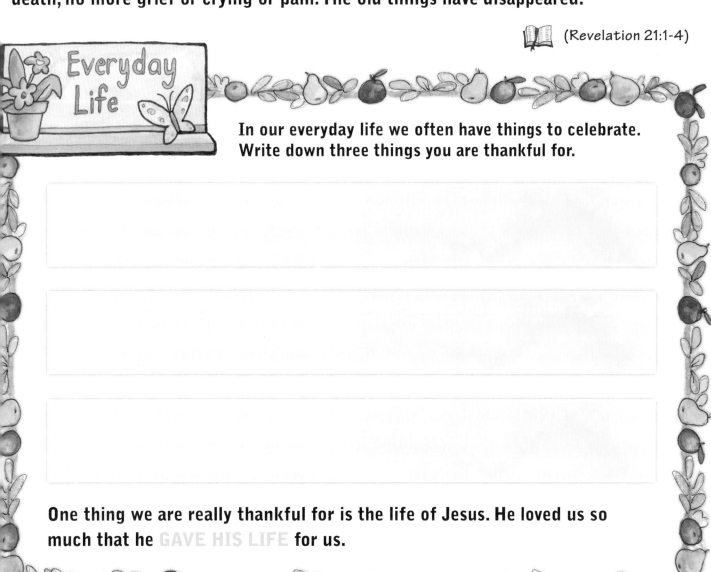

Everyday Life

In our everyday life we often have things to celebrate. Write down three things you are thankful for.

One thing we are really thankful for is the life of Jesus. He loved us so much that he GAVE HIS LIFE for us.

When Jesus celebrated the Passover at his very LAST SUPPER **he said the bread and wine was** HIMSELF. **The wine was his life, which he was giving for us.**

Jesus called the hard times of his life a cup of sorrow.

Once he asked his friends if they could drink some of this cup with him. He said that if they could drink his cup of sorrow, they would rule with him in his kingdom. If we are strong and stand up for what is right we might find it hard at first, but in the end we will be proud of ourselves. We will see that we are helping to bring about God's everlasting party –

THE ETERNAL BANQUET.

In the Eucharist we are united to the unselfish love of Jesus in giving up his life for his friends. "No one has greater love than to give up his life for his friends." This is exactly what Jesus did.

A word search. Find the words below.

CUP   FEAST   PARTY   LOVE   BRANCHES
VINE
KINGDOM   HAPPINESS   WINE   DRINK

```
L O V E Z M H A P P I N E S S J
V C I Z Y P L K A Y T R Q W X J
K I N G D O M F R F X K N I R D
G H E M P P S W T S A E F H G D
B D F W U G H K Y L K Y T D C V
S E H C N A R B Y H J K E N I W
```

91

Family Time

Surround this prayer with happy pictures of our beautiful world. You could have sad pictures as well, showing what still needs to be done to bring about the kingdom of God: a world of peace and justice. **Cut out pictures from magazines, draw, or write in the shapes of the frame.**

Heavenly Father,
you give us all the good things in life.
You give us food to give us strength and drink to refresh us.
When we eat together and drink together we grow closer to one another and to you.
Blessed are you, Lord, God of all creation.
Amen.

Chapter Nine

Do this in memory of me

We have lots of different kinds of meals.

We have

(CUBEBEARS)

We have

(KATE WAYAS)

We have

(MAIFLY MELAS)

We have

(CIPNICS)

We have

(RATPIES)

A really good meal is one where we enjoy the food and enjoy the company. **We are changed for the better after a really good meal.**

Draw a picture of a really good meal you had. Can you remember what you ate and drank? Can you remember who was there? Can you remember what you talked about?

The Old Testament

We have been thinking a lot about Moses and how he led the people of God out of slavery. At last came the great night when God finally led the people to freedom.

It was in the springtime and there was a full moon. Moses told the people to have a meal together before they went, as the journey to freedom would be long and hard. The meal had to be eaten quickly, so there was no time to bake bread with yeast. They had to eat unleavened bread.

Each family offered a perfect young lamb to God, and ate all of it themselves or with their neighbours.

Moses told the people they must always celebrate this **PASSOVER** meal. By having this meal, they would make the wonder of that night live again. It would remind them that God was their **SAVIOUR**, and it would make their salvation very real.

The New Testament

Jesus celebrated the PASSOVER every year. When he was a boy he asked questions about it, and learnt what it all meant. He realised how important it was.

It celebrated how the people of God were saved from sin and death. Their lives were changed from lives of slavery to lives of freedom.

Jesus spent his whole life telling people how much his Father loved them. It is difficult to understand that some people hated him. These people decided to kill him. Jesus knew he was going to die. The reason he had come from heaven was to give his life for us. This was how he was going to save us. By dying and rising from the dead he showed us that death and evil had no power over him, and need have no power over us.

Jesus is the new

Lamb of God.

Jesus didn't just give his life for us years ago when he died on Calvary. He gives us his new risen life now. He did this by changing the PASSOVER feast into the EUCHARIST.

The EUCHARIST is the transformed PASSOVER of the greatly enlarged people of God.

Jesus is the new LAMB OF GOD who saves everyone and brings everyone life.

The Last Supper

The night before he died, Jesus celebrated the Passover feast with his friends. He wanted to show them how much he loved them. Judas, who was going to betray Jesus, was also there. This didn't stop Jesus from being completely full of love. While they were at table he took bread, blessed it, broke it, and gave it to his friends.

He told them to...

TAKE – EAT.
THIS IS MY BODY.
Then he took the wine. He gave thanks, and told them to share the cup. He said,

TAKE – DRINK.
THIS IS MY BLOOD.
He told them to do what he had done. Whenever they did this, Jesus would be really there, as food and drink from heaven.

Communion:
This is the moment when we receive Jesus under the appearance of bread and wine.

Eucharistic Prayer: A prayer praising God; calling down the Holy Spirit; retelling the Last Supper story; and with the words of Jesus, changing the bread into his body and the wine into his blood. ✔ P.134

Colour this picture of the Last Supper and draw yourself into the blank space.

Church

At the Eucharist we remember and join in with the **Last Supper of Jesus.**

The priest takes [_____] **and** [_____] **and says the same words that Jesus said.**

TAKE AND EAT – TAKE AND DRINK
THIS IS MY BODY – THIS MY BLOOD

The bread isn't ordinary bread any more.
It is Jesus – the bread of life.

The wine isn't ordinary wine any more.
It is the life of Christ.
When we share the meal of the Eucharist we are sharing in the life of Christ. Jesus gives himself to us as food and drink.

Why do you think he did this?
He changed bread and wine into himself because he wanted to give us his...

 (efil)

Ordinary food and drink is very important for us because it makes us strong in our bodies.

Last Supper:
The special meal which Jesus shared with his friends the night before he died. ✔ P.135

Host:
The bread that is used in the Mass after it becomes the body of the Lord Jesus. ✔ P.135

The food and drink Jesus gives us makes us strong to LOVE. LOVE is the most important reason why Jesus gives us himself in the Eucharist.

- He loves us.
- He wants us to love him and everyone.

THE **LAMB** OF **GOD**

The early Israelites kept flocks of sheep and goats. They thought of a lamb as something pure and innocent: as good a gift as possible to offer to God.

JESUS is the pure and innocent one.
JESUS is the gift God gives to us.
JESUS is the gift God accepts from us.
JESUS is the "Lamb of God".
He is the perfect gift.

At Communion in the Mass (Eucharist) we offer each other the:

Sign of peace:
A sign of love and friendship, usually a handshake, by which we wish one another the peace of Christ.

The congregation then sings together:

Lamb of God, you take away the sins of the world, have mercy on us.

Lamb of God, you take away the sins of the world, have mercy on us.

Lamb of God, you take away the sins of the world, grant us peace.

Everyday Life

If we share in the life of Christ in the Eucharist, it means we can live like Christ every day.

You are probably trying to live loving lives already, because you are children of God.

When you receive Jesus in the Eucharist you are changed. You will have more strength for the journey of life, just as Moses and his people had strength for their journey to the Promised Land.

You will have more strength to love as Jesus does.

When you receive Jesus in the Eucharist you will be just as close to Jesus as his friends were at the Last Supper.

This means that no matter what problems you have to face in life, Jesus is with you. He feeds you with himself, so you have his life, his strength, his power. You have the life and love of Christ in you.

Here is a word search. Find these words.

LAST SUPPER

TAKE MOSES WINE MEAL CALVARY

PASSOVER BREAD JESUS EAT

```
P L A S T S U P P E R N P S S T
V M E A L P L L R E V O S S A P
B R E A D E W G R T A K E K R K
C A L V A R Y G A G X C L A P J
B L F T U G N U D A E R E N I W
J E S U S A E A T H J S E S O M
```

Family Time

Something to think about with your family.

Jesus is really present to us in the bread and wine. Under the signs of bread and wine he is sharing himself, his love and his life, totally and completely.

Our Lady's chapel:
A place in many churches dedicated to Mary, the Mother of God.

Rosary:
A circle of beads is held in the hand while a prayer is said at each bead. The prayers are simple: the "Lord's Prayer", the "Hail Mary" and "Glory Be". While praying we think of events in the life of Jesus.

Jesus offers himself to us, to be taken by each one of us into our hearts and lives – into the lives of all who believe in him.

FAMILY PRAYER – to say together

Thank you, Lord God, for our parents and all they do for us.
Thank you, Lord God, for our children; may we recognise and acknowledge you in each of them.
Thank you, Lord God, for all the people who show us love and care: (think of names).
Thank you, Lord God, for the smiling faces around us and all the friends you give us.
For each person that brings us closer to you: (think of names) we thank you, Lord. **Amen.**

Jesus is not present "just to be there". He gives himself to us to be accepted by us, so that he may truly live in us and we in him.

Chapter Ten

Body of Christ

DO YOU KNOW?

Tabernacle:
A special decorated container or safe, in which the Blessed Sacrament is reserved. The consecrated hosts will be used for sick and housebound people. It is in a prominent place in church.

Body of Christ:
A name for Holy Communion and also for the family of the Church. ✔ P.134

Blessed Sacrament:
The real presence of Jesus in the form of consecrated bread. ✔ P.134

Good Friday:
Christians remember Jesus' crucifixion on Good Friday – "God's Friday". We say prayers together as we remember Jesus' suffering; we say prayers asking God to help anyone who suffers.

Sanctuary light:
A small lamp, either white or red, placed near the tabernacle.

Easter Sunday:
Christians celebrate the resurrection of Jesus from the dead. It is the most special day in the Church's calendar when we show our happiness and hope in the power of God.

Have you ever seen a tadpole turning into a frog?

First the back legs grow. Then the front legs grow.
Its long tadpole tail disappears.
Soon it can hop and live on land.
The same life is inside the little
creature, but it looks
completely
different on the outside.

Caterpillars change as
well.
At first the caterpillar is
fat and crawly. It creeps
along branches
and twigs. Sometimes it
falls to
the ground.
After sleeping in a
cocoon it rises to
a new life as a
butterfly.

Colour in this butterfly with its beautiful new wings.

You have also changed on the outside since you were born. The change in you is a gradual change. Now you are taller and stronger than when you were a baby. But you probably feel the same inside as you did a few years ago. You are the same person.

The Old Testament

We do not have an Old Testament story this time. Today we will focus on the New Testament.

For Christians all the Old Testament stories are getting us ready for the New Testament. Today you are having **TWO** stories from the New Testament. They are both true stories about after Jesus had died and been buried. They are about

JESUS RISEN FROM THE DEAD.

The New Testament

Last time we talked about the day before Jesus died. He gave himself to his friends as food and drink at his Last Supper. The next day he was put to death on the cross. That was Good Friday.

Jesus died on Good Friday. He was still dead on the Saturday. His friends were very, very sad. They thought Jesus was gone for ever. But on the third day – on the Sunday – lots of people suddenly saw him alive again. He looked so different that they did not recognise him. Here is the first story we know about Jesus appearing to someone after he had risen from the dead.

Mary and the gardener

Mary from Magdala was very upset when Jesus died because she loved Jesus very much.

On the third day after Jesus had died, while it was still dark, Mary decided to go to the tomb where Jesus lay. When she got there she saw that the stone over the opening had been rolled back, and the tomb was empty. This upset her even more, because she thought the soldiers had taken away the body of Jesus.

Mary stood weeping outside the tomb. She bent down and, looking inside, saw two angels sitting there. "Why are you weeping?" they asked her.

"Because they have taken Jesus away, and I don't know where he is," she sobbed.

Then she turned round, and saw someone standing there. She thought it was the gardener. The stranger asked her why she was crying.
"Who are you looking for?" he said.

"Have you taken Jesus away?" she asked. The stranger looked at Mary with love.
"Mary!" he said.

Straight away Mary recognised him. He wasn't a stranger. He wasn't the gardener. He was Jesus, alive with a new risen life. A better life than before.

"Master!" cried Mary. She then went back to the rest of the disciples, and told them that she had seen the Lord. Jesus was alive.

(Adapted from John 20:11-18)

Mary didn't recognise Jesus because he looked very different with his new risen life.

There is another story about two friends of Jesus who didn't recognise Jesus when he rose from the dead on page 112.

The two friends and the stranger

Two friends of Jesus were running away from Jerusalem. They were very upset that Jesus had died. They thought Jesus was going to be a great leader, like Moses or King David.

As they were walking along, a stranger joined them, and asked what they were talking about. They told him all about Jesus dying, and how disappointed they were that Jesus had not freed the people.

"Oh you foolish people!" said the stranger, and he began to explain the Old Testament, and how it linked up with Jesus.

The friends listened excitedly to everything the stranger said. When they got to their village, they didn't want the stranger to leave them. "Stay here with us for the night," they said. "It's getting dark." While they were at table, the stranger took bread. He blessed it and broke it and gave it to them. All at once they recognised him. It wasn't a stranger. It was Jesus – alive with his new risen life.

As soon as they recognised him, Jesus disappeared. But the friends were no longer afraid. "We should have realised," they said.

"All the time he was talking to us along the road our hearts were burning inside us. Jesus looks different on the outside with his new risen life, but inside it is the very same Jesus."

Straight away the two friends hurried back to Jerusalem, and joined the rest of their friends there.

"It is true," everyone said. "Jesus has really risen from the dead."

 (Adapted from Luke 24:13-35)

When we go to the Eucharist we really and truly meet Jesus, just as Mary Magdalene did, and just as the two friends did.

Jesus isn't there with a physical body, like the one he had before he died, but we really do meet him in a special way when we go to Communion.

It is the same Jesus, who died for us and rose again, but he is with us by the power of the Holy Spirit, who makes Jesus present in the consecrated bread and wine.

When the priest says the words of consecration,
"This is my Body",
"This is the chalice of my Blood",
the Holy Spirit enters the bread and wine with the risen life of Christ.
When we receive the consecrated bread the priest says,
"The Body of Christ."
We say, **"Amen."** *(Yes, I believe.)*
When we receive
the chalice the priest says,
"The Blood of Christ."
We say,
"Amen." *(Yes, I believe.)*

Consecration:
By the power of the Holy Spirit, the bread and wine are changed into the Body and Blood of Christ, when the priest says, "This is my Body"; "This is my Blood".

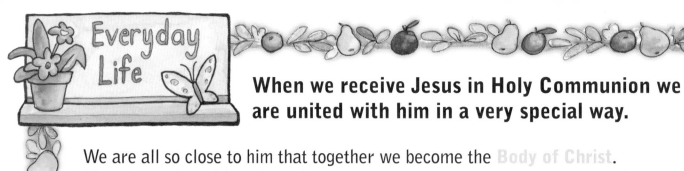

When we receive Jesus in Holy Communion we are united with him in a very special way.

We are all so close to him that together we become the Body of Christ. This means that although on the outside we may look just the same as before, by receiving Holy Communion we are changed. We have the risen life of Christ in us. WE ARE THE BODY OF CHRIST.

Jesus still had the marks of his wounds when he rose from the dead. After receiving the Eucharist we may feel wonderful, we may feel ordinary or we may feel we are weak and wounded.

But no matter how you feel when you receive Jesus in the Eucharist, you know that he is deep inside your being. He loves you even more than you can possibly realise.

After receiving Jesus, try to keep still and quiet. You can talk to him in your own words, or just enjoy recognising he is with you.

Finish the prayer with something you may like to say to Jesus.

Dear Jesus,
thank you for coming to me in the Eucharist...

_____

_____

_____

Next time we meet, we will be thinking about all we can do to carry on the Good News that Jesus gives us.

For now, here is a word search. Find all these words.

CHANGE LIFE FAITH RECOGNISE BELIEVE
RISEN SPIRIT AMEN CHRIST

```
E  V  E  I  L  E  B  Q  W  C  H  R  I  S  T  R
H  Y  G  T  I  R  I  P  S  G  H  J  K  L  P  P
Q  W  N  Z  X  I  W  N  B  X  S  S  E  D  H  J
F  K  A  B  V  S  Z  M  B  H  T  I  A  F  T  R
H  J  H  M  N  E  X  L  K  X  C  Z  W  Q  I  W
R  E  C  O  G  N  I  S  E  G  J  N  E  M  A  L
```

 **Family Time**

I shall be celebrating my First Holy Communion...

on [   ]   at [   ]

Date   *Time & Place*

These are some people I would like to invite to be with me to share my special day:

_____

_____

_____

_____

_____

Chapter Eleven

To love and to serve

Concluding Rites

Everyday Life

Every day you are blessed to have something to eat.
Draw your favourite food and drink.

If you don't eat you feel _____ (weka)

You might even _____ (fanit)

Draw you feeling weak before a meal and full of energy after a meal.

Me feeling weak before a meal. : Me full of energy after a meal.

~The Promised Land~

The Old Testament

We have spent a long time thinking about how Moses helped the people of God escape from slavery. In the desert the people were fed by God to give them strength for the journey. At last they reached the Promised Land. Joshua was the leader by then, so Joshua led the people to freedom. Joshua is the same name as Jesus.

The name means SAVIOUR.

The people of God settled in the Promised Land. It was so wonderful after the desert that they said it was a land flowing with milk and honey. There was plenty to eat and drink for everyone. The people of God always tried to be kind to poor people and to strangers. They remembered that once they had been poor travellers, with nowhere to live. When they forgot to think of others, the prophets reminded them.
Jesus is a prophet, but he is much more than a prophet.

Jesus is the SON OF GOD.

The New Testament

Jesus, the **Son of God**, spent his life on earth showing us how to live as children of God. Jesus was always kind to people who were poor. He healed those who were sick, fed those who were hungry, he told everyone how much his Father loved them.

After he rose from the dead he carried on loving everyone. Here is a story of how he fed his friends when they were tired and hungry.

One evening Peter was bored. He said to his friends, "I'm going fishing." His friends said, "We'll come with you." They got their old boat out and dragged it onto the lake. They fished all night, but they couldn't catch anything. Not even an old sandal! When the sunrise came they were cold and hungry. They decided to go home. They were very disappointed. Now they would have to buy some food for their breakfast.

They could see a stranger on the shore. The stranger called out to them, "Have you caught anything?"

"No," they called back to the stranger.

"Cast your net on the other side of the boat," shouted the stranger. "Then you will find some fish."

They cast their net, and, to their surprise, they caught so many fish that they could not pull the net on board.

"It's the Lord!" shouted John. When Peter heard this, he jumped overboard to get to Jesus. When everyone else had landed, they noticed that Jesus had a fire already lit, and he was cooking a lovely breakfast for them on the beach.

Jesus took the bread and gave it to them. He gave them some fish. They knew it was Jesus feeding them. Then Jesus asked Peter three times if he loved him. Peter said yes, and Jesus told him to feed his lambs and sheep.

The lambs and sheep of Jesus are all the poor, weak people of the world. Jesus asks his friends to look after them all.

 (Adapted from John 21:1-17)

Colour this picture of Jesus with food for his friends at the seaside.

Family Time

A WAY TO PRAY

Before you begin this prayer, make yourselves comfortable.
Close your eyes and imagine Jesus looking at you. Jesus says, "Let your light shine."
Think about all the people you know who shine with the light and love of Christ.
Thank Jesus for his trust in us to be his body here on earth.

A PRAYER
TO SAY TOGETHER

Christ has no body now on earth but ours,
no hands but ours,
no feet but ours.
Ours are the eyes through which is to shine out
Christ's compassion on the world.
Ours are the feet through which he is to go about doing good.
Ours are the hands with which he is to bless all people NOW.

Please help each one of us, Jesus,
to be your body here on earth.
Thank you. **Amen.** (St Teresa of Avila)

Look out for ways in which you can now take part in your church and in the life of your parish: you will be **VERY** welcome!

Church

At the end of the Eucharist, the priest or deacon will give one of several directions. You can find all of them on p. 133. The simplest of them is:

"Go in peace."
With the peace of the Lord we go out to love and serve the Lord. We have been fed by our Good Shepherd. Now we have a chance to show how much we love him: by following his example, loving and serving everyone we meet.

Here are some ways you can love and serve the Lord during the week:

Do the gardening

Help someone older than you

Visit someone
who is sick

Look after the dog

Write a letter saying thank you to your
prayer sponsor (or godparent) for praying
for you. **Here is some help with ideas and spelling.**

Dear _____

Thank you very much for praying for me.

enjoyed   First Holy Communion   lovely weather   excited
nervous   very happy   family   relations   presents   tired

I hope you are keeping well

Love

Here is a word search. Find these words.

HAPPINESS **CHRIST** **STRENGTH** **LOVE**
LORD **LIFE** **CONTENTMENT**

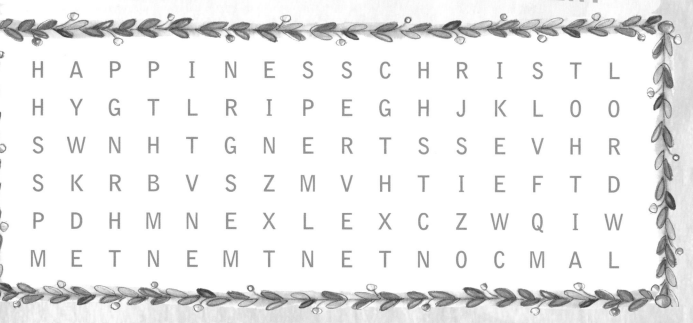

```
H A P P I N E S S C H R I S T L
H Y G T L R I P E G H J K L O O
S W N H T G N E R T S S E V H R
S K R B V S Z M V H T I E F T D
P D H M N E X L E X C Z W Q I W
M E T N E M T N E T N O C M A L
```

Thanks be to God

127

Make this page special by adding bits of your own. You could add pages and pages of things if you wanted to. It could be a place where you collect prayers and ideas about God and people and everything God has made.

My Prayers

Sign of the Cross
In the name of the Father,
and of the Son,
and of the Holy Spirit.
Amen.

The Lord's Prayer
Our Father, who art in heaven,
hallowed be thy name;
thy kingdom come,
thy will be done
on earth as it is in heaven.
Give us this day our daily bread,
and forgive us our trespasses,
as we forgive those who trespass against us;
and lead us not into temptation,
but deliver us from evil.
Amen.

Hail Mary

Hail, Mary, full of grace,
the Lord is with thee.
Blessed art thou among women,
and blessed is the fruit
of thy womb, Jesus.
Holy Mary, Mother of God,
pray for us sinners,
now and at the hour of our death.
Amen.

Glory be to the Father

Glory be to the Father and to the Son and to the Holy Spirit.
As it was in the beginning, is now, and ever shall be,
world without end.
Amen.

Grace before Meals

Thank you, Lord, for this food
and for those who prepared it.
Bless us as we share your gifts.
Amen.

Prayer of Thanksgiving

Thank you, Lord, for all your gifts to me.
Help me to use them in your service.
Amen.

Renewal of Baptismal Promises

Let us renew the promises of Holy Baptism, by which we once renounced Satan and his works and promised to serve God in the holy Catholic Church. And so I ask you:

Priest: Do you renounce Satan?
People: **I do.**
Priest: And all his works?
People: **I do.**
Priest: And all his empty show?
People: **I do.**

Priest: Do you believe in God, the Father almighty, Creator of heaven and earth?
People: **I do.**

Priest: Do you believe in Jesus Christ, his only Son, our Lord, who was born of the Virgin Mary, suffered death and was buried, rose again from the dead and is seated at the right hand of the Father?
People: **I do.**

Priest: Do you believe in the Holy Spirit, the holy Catholic Church, the communion of saints, the forgiveness of sins, the resurrection of the body, and life everlasting?
People: **I do.**

Priest: And may almighty God, the Father of our Lord Jesus Christ, who has given us new birth by water and the Holy Spirit, and bestowed on us forgiveness of our sins, keep us by his grace, in Christ Jesus our Lord, for eternal life. **Amen.**

Penitential Act

> **Priest or deacon:** …Lord, have mercy *or* Kyrie, eleison.
> **People: Lord, have mercy** *or* **Kyrie, eleison.**
> **Priest or deacon:** …Christ, have mercy *or* Christe, eleison.
> **People: Christ, have mercy** *or* **Christe, eleison.**
> **Priest or deacon:** …Lord, have mercy *or* Kyrie, eleison.
> **People: Lord, have mercy** *or* **Kyrie, eleison.**

The Liturgy of the Word

After the first (and second) reading:
> **Reader:** The word of the Lord.
> **People: Thanks be to God.**

Before the Gospel:
> **Priest or deacon:** The Lord be with you.
> **People: And with your spirit.**
> **Priest or deacon:** A reading from the holy Gospel according to…
> **People: Glory to you, O Lord.**

After the reading of the Gospel:
> **Priest or deacon:** The Gospel of the Lord.
> **People: Praise to you, Lord Jesus Christ.**

Eucharistic Acclamation

> **Priest:** The mystery of faith:
>
> **People: We proclaim your Death, O Lord,
> and profess your Resurrection
> until you come again.**

or

People: **When we eat this Bread and drink this Cup,**
we proclaim your Death, O Lord,
until you come again.

or

People: **Save us, Saviour of the world,**
for by your Cross and Resurrection
you have set us free.

The sign of peace

Priest or deacon: The peace of the Lord be with you always.
People: **And with your spirit.**

The priest or deacon invites the people to give the sign of peace.

Priest or deacon: Let us offer each other the sign of peace.

At Mass we usually exchange a sign of peace by shaking hands with those around us.

Just before Communion

All: **Lord, I am not worthy**
that you should enter under my roof,
but only say the word
and my soul shall be healed.

Dismissal

Priest or deacon:

Go forth, the Mass is ended.

or

Go and announce the Gospel of the Lord.

or

Go in peace, glorifying the Lord by your life.

or

Go in peace.

People: **Thanks be to God.**

Special Words

Baptism: The sacrament through which I became a member of God's Christian family, the Church and through which I was cleansed of original sin.

Blessed Sacrament: The real presence of Jesus in the form of consecrated bread.

Body of Christ: A name for Holy Communion and also for the family of the Church.

Bread of life: A name for the sacrament of Jesus in Holy Communion.

Christian: Christian is the name given to followers of Christ.

Eucharist: Comes from a Greek word meaning "to give thanks". It is often used for the Mass, and the body and blood of Jesus in particular.

Eucharistic Prayer: A prayer praising God; calling down the Holy Spirit; retelling the Last Supper story; and with the words of Jesus, changing the bread into his body and the wine into his blood.

Special Words

Host: The bread that is used in the Mass after it becomes the body of the Lord Jesus.

Lamb of God: A name Christians give to Jesus.

Last Supper: The special meal which Jesus shared with his friends the night before he died.

Liturgy: The worship of God in public prayer. The liturgy of the Church is made up of ceremonies for which there are clear guidelines.

Mass: Also called the Eucharist – the celebration of the death and resurrection of Jesus.

Sacrifice: Means "to offer". During the Mass, the priest, in the name of the people, makes present again Christ's offering of himself to the Father. We recognise that Jesus is Lord and Saviour and that we believe in him.

These people were present to celebrate my
First Communion Day with me

I received **Holy Communion** for the first time

on:

at:

celebrant:

my catechist:

my parent/s:

I Belong

First Holy Communion Programme

Published by **Redemptorist Publications**
A Registered Charity Limited by guarantee.
Registered in England 03261721.

Text: Aileen Urquhart
Additional text: Yvonne Fordyce and Alison Jones

Illustration © Finola Stack
Design: Chris Nutbeen
Editor: Yvonne Fordyce

First published March 1998
Revised edition August 2002
Reprinted March 2008
Second revised edition September 2010
Reprinted July 2012
Reprinted March 2015
Reprinted February 2017
Reprinted January 2020

ISBN 978-0-85231-377-0

A CIP catalogue record for this book is available from the British Library.

Printed and bound in China through Colorcraft Ltd, Hong Kong.

Wolf's Lane, Chawton, Hampshire GU34 3HQ
Tel: 01420 88222 **email:** rp@rpbooks.co.uk **web:** www.rpbooks.co.uk